SONGS IN SEASON

NEW WORDS FOR WORSHIP TO FAMILIAR TUNES

— ROD HORSFIELD —

COVENTRY PRESS

Published in Australia by
Coventry Press
33 Scoresby Road
Bayswater VIC 3153

ISBN 9781922589293

Copyright © Rod Horsfield 2023

All rights reserved. Other than for the purposes and subject to the conditions prescribed under the *Copyright Act*, no part of this publication may be reproduced, stored in a retrieval system, or transmitted in any form or by any means, electronic, mechanical, photocopying, recording or otherwise, without the prior permission of the publisher.

Scripture quotations are from the *New Revised Standard Version Bible*, copyright 1989, Division of Christian Education of the National Council of the Churches of Christ in the United States of America. Used by permission. All rights reserved.

Catalogue-in-Publication entry is available from the National Library of Australia
http://catalogue.nla.gov.au

Cover design by Ian James – www.jgd.com.au
Images copyright Ken Rookes 2023 - ken@kenrookes.com.au
Text design by Coventry Press
Set in EB Garamond

Printed in Australia

Contents

Foreword 7
Introduction 8
Acknowledgments 10

GATHERING SONGS 13

1. A gathering song 15
2. Awake, awake 16
3. God, we gather 17
4. In this holy space 18
5. Invocation #1 19
6. Invocation #2 20
7. Jesus be among us 21
8. We gather together 22

HYMNS OF PRAISE 23

9. A hymn of praise 25
10. Glory be to God 26
11. The God of history 27
12. We praise you, God 28

CONFESSION and FORGIVENESS — 29

13. No condemnation now — 31
14. We are forgiven — 32

PRAYER — 33

15. A lament (after Psalm 6) — 35
16. As Jesus taught Us — 36
17. Jesus, Son of Mary — 37
18. Who am I (after Psalm 131) — 38

PROCLAMATION — 39

19. Gift of grace — 41
20. The Apostles' Creed — 43

SACRAMENTS — 45

21. New life in Christ — 47
22. Shall we gather at the table — 48

DISCIPLESHIP — 51

23. Jesus was a stranger — 53
24. Love is service — 54
25. O God, forgive — 55
26. O God of love and justice — 56
27. The call to discipleship — 57

BLESSING and DISMISSAL   59

28. A life that sings   61
29. Go with us, Lord   62

ADVENT and CHRISTMAS   63

30. Advent/Christmas doxology   65
31. Joseph's carol   66
32. The child Jesus   67
33. What child is this   68

LECTIONARY SONGS   71

34. Transfiguration song (for children)   73
35. Evening prayer   74
36. Ascension introit   75
37. Holy Spirit fire #1   76
38. Holy Spirit fire #2   77
39. Pentecost invocation   79
40. Through the artistry of children   80

Foreword

During his years of ministry in the Uniting Church, Rod Horsfield has been consistently committed to lively and faithful worship. He also has a deep interest in poetry. In more recent years, having laid aside the responsibilities of full-time ministry, Rod has devoted more time to the writing of hymns. I have had the privilege of commenting on many of his hymns.

In reading and singing them, I have been struck by the facility with which Rod is able to express biblical ideas in clear modern language. I am sure that those who sing these hymns will find their faith and understanding enriched.

The *Basis of Union* says that the Uniting Church 'prays that it may be ready when occasion demands to confess the Lord in fresh words and deeds' (para.11, 1992 edition). Rod's work is a good example of that commitment.

Together in Song was published in 1999, so Rod's hymns are too recent for that publication; however, his prize-winning hymn 'Before you, God, we dare to sing' is included in the TIS supplement *Songs of Grace* (2018). It is to be hoped that, in time, his hymns will be as widely sung as those of the notable Australian hymn-writers and song-writers Geoff Bullock, James McAuley, Robin Mann and Elizabeth Smith.

Revd Dr D'Arcy Wood

[*Former President of the UCA Assembly (1991-1994), scholar, ecumenist, musician, liturgist, was one of the editors of* The Australian Hymn Book (1977), Uniting in Worship (1988), *and* Together in Song (1999).]

Introduction

These hymns and songs were written by a minister of Word and Sacraments of the Uniting Church in Australia for worship by congregations. For nearly a lifetime, I have been committed to the UCA's Constitutional declaration that 'The primary expression of the corporate life of the Church shall be the Congregation' [Constitution 22]. I also remain convinced that the faithful worship of congregations is essential to the health and vitality of a Christian community at mission in a rapidly changing cultural context.

In these times of the decline of Christendom and the search for fresh expressions of church, it is important that Christians do not 'throw the baby out with the bath water'. In my view, congregational worship needs to be both traditional and contemporary. The task of Christian communities is to reinterpret the tradition so that its fundamental truth speaks into, and is enacted in, their contemporary context. It is important that the Church does not lose what is essential about Christian faith in its search for cultural relevance. To do so, would mean it would lose its distinctive message for the culture it wants to engage in the struggle for belief.

In writing new hymns and songs, I believe that in worship, the people both address, and are addressed by, a God who has chosen to enter human life and history. In the conversation of worship, people praise the God who has so acted **as well as** listen for the Word of God addressed to them both communally and individually. People also bring the elements and experiences of their own lives in the contemporary world and offer them to God.

In writing new words to known tunes, I hope these songs will make the following contributions to contemporary worship.

1. Celebrate the important beliefs of the Christian faith.
2. Inspire the worship of the Trinitarian God.
3. Express fundamental theological convictions in new ways.
4. Encourage people to express emotion through words and music.

5. Strengthen artful worship as a communal activity of the whole people of God.
6. Encourage the use of new songs to enliven people's experience of the liturgy.
7. Provide words that enlarge the congregation's repertoire of words and music.
8. Encourage people to rediscover the use of hymns as poetry in individual devotion.

May these musical words provide a way to sing the Lord's song in the strange land the world has become for the people of God in these times.

Rod Horsfield
All Saints Day
1 November 2022

> ... but be filled with the Spirit, as you sing psalms and hymns and spiritual songs among yourselves, singing and making melody to the Lord in your hearts... Ephesians 5:8-19

Acknowledgments

As a writer of words and with no musical training, I am indebted to many people who helped put my words to music, which is the key to congregations being able to offer worship that inspires and nourishes the people. The first were the people of West End Methodist Mission in Brisbane whose enthusiastic and participatory worship enabled a naïve teenager to feel, in the gathered community, something of the presence of God that awakened his curiosity and nourished his quest for faith.

All of the congregations in which I have had responsibility for leading the worship have contributed to the songs gathered here. The people at Pilgrim Uniting Church, Launceston, provided fertile ground for me to experiment with 'blended worship'. Together, we created a band and singing group, working with the organist on the historic pipe organ, to curate worship that was both traditional and contemporary. They demonstrated each Sunday that it is the active participation of the people of the gathered community, using all their gifts, who make worship the inspirational experience in communicating the grace of God that it should be.

I have to say quite simply that the inspiration to try and provide words for people to sing in church has come from being a member of a community trying to celebrate and integrate the profound truth of the Christian faith that is both inspirational and relevant.

I am grateful to Ken Rookes, an artist and poet in his own right, who has provided relief prints for each of the sections of the book. In worship, in which we human beings are often too wordy, Ken's images are reminders that human beings are not the only part of creation that praises the Creator of all things. I appreciate the playful spirit he has brought to my request to provide images for this book of words and music.

I am grateful to D'Arcy Wood who checked the scansion of my words and rhythms and suggested alternative tunes from *Together in Song* to carry my words. He has also kindly written the Foreword.

I owe a debt to Hugh McGinlay from Coventry Press who first thought my words were worth sharing and who became my diligent and creative editor.

Over the years, I have learned in workshops and educational courses with Brian Wren, Robin Mann and John Bell. I find continuing inspiration in the work of Elizabeth Smith and Shirley Murray in particular.

This volume is dedicated to all gathered communities who are eager to learn how they may learn to 'sing a new song to the Lord' (Psalm 148) and be enriched in worship by doing so.

Rod Horsfield

GATHERING SONGS

Apostle Birds

Gathering as one
they come
to share their common life

1
A GATHERING SONG

Lord, as we gather here,
each called from our own place,
form us as your community
and serve us with your grace.

We come in poverty
unsure of how to ask
your mercy on our sinfulness
our failure in our tasks.

We wait upon your Word
its ancient truth proclaimed
and through the living Word made flesh
salvation is attained.

And is the table spread?
Are sinners to be fed
and given for their holiness
the Lord's own wine and bread?

Received as your beloved,
fed, nurtured and forgiven,
Lord, with your blessing send us out
to live the life of heaven.

Tune: Franconia TiS 490

> Christian worship is not a gathering of individuals, each coming to have 'their spiritual needs' met. It is a communal activity requiring the 'full, conscious and active participation of the people'. We are gathered by God as a community to be served by God through Word and Sacraments. We are not present to watch a performance so that we may 'have our spiritual batteries recharged'. This hymn seeks to celebrate the fundamental structure of Christian worship.

2

AWAKE, AWAKE

Awake, awake to worship God
for now the time has come
when God's salvation light will dawn
and shine on every one
the warmth and glory of his grace
in God's incarnate Son.

Awake, you people of the Lord,
prepare your voice to greet
the One who comes with healing word
in humble majesty;
to be within our company
through Word and Sacrament.

Awake, awake, to hear again
the call to follow him;
to spend yourself nor count the cost
to serve the least of them
for whom the Son of God has come
to share humanity.

Tune: Sheltered Dale (*Methodist Hymn Book* 588)

This hymn is inspired by one written by the First World War Padre Geoffrey Studdert Kennedy (Woodbine Willie) and published in the Methodist Hymn Book. Kennedy wrote poems from the trenches that were highly popular in the 20th century. I have written this hymn as a Call to Worship using one of his lines (line 3, verse 3) as a call for people to pay attention to the God who comes and addresses us in worship.

3
GOD, WE GATHER

God, we gather as your people
seeking wisdom from your Word,
warm our hearts, life-giving Spirit,
free our minds, O gracious Lord.

Tune our voices to your music,
silence all infernal noise,
breathe your peace into our meeting
show us ways to harmonise.

Help us to discern your presence
God, the holy Mystery;
recognising Jesus with us
in a holy company.

Tune: TiS 101: Omni Die

THE BASIS OF UNION
Paragraph 4

(a) The Congregation is the embodiment in one place of the One Holy Catholic and Apostolic Church, worshipping, witnessing and serving as a fellowship of the Spirit in Christ. Its members meet regularly to hear God's Word, to celebrate the sacraments, to build one another up in love, to share in the wider responsibilities of the Church, and to serve the world...

4
IN THIS HOLY SPACE

Come gather, God's people, in this holy space,
where faithful disciples have sung out God's praise;
lift voices and hearts with the earth's salty tears
and enter the mystery of the God beyond years.

Come stand though uncertain with doubts lurking near
and the powers of destruction provoking our fear;
depend on God's promise, his word is secure,
in the palm of his hand, we are held safe and sure.

Tune: TiS 143 St Denio

> This hymn celebrates that worship is done by people who come together, bringing the elements of their personal lives with them into that time and space. They join with an historic company that is continuous through history. The local saints are included but let us not forget 'the whole company of heaven' too. In this kind of worship, we are served by a God who has promised to be with us, and to nurture us in the truth of God's revelation in Jesus Christ.

GATHERING SONGS

5
INVOCATION #1

Jesus be among us
   in your risen power;
may we who are fearful
   know your presence here.

Help us lift our voices,
   tune discordant hearts
that our time of worship
   may your life impart.

May your Holy Spirit
   teach us to depend
on the intercession
   of the Risen One.

Tune Tis 600 (ii) North Coates

> The secular meaning of the word 'invocation' is the act of appealing to a higher authority for help. In a liturgical setting, 'invocation' is a prayer to God for help or blessing at the beginning of a service. An Invocation at the beginning of worship also helps people to clear their hearts and minds of clutter and preoccupations in preparation for worship. It is a reminder that we can ask the Spirit of God to help us prepare to encounter the grace of God in worship.

6
INVOCATION #2

Holy Spirit prompt us as we come to pray;
loosen up our tongues, inspire the words we say:
stir indifferent hearts and calm our anxious haste;
give us songs to sing the wonders of your grace.

Tune: Glenfinlas TiS 600 (i)
or North Coates Tis 600 (ii)

This invocation is a 'breathing in' hymn when, at the beginning worship, we ask the Spirit's help to calm our hearts and enliven our bodies so that we may open all of our selves to the giving and receiving between us and God that is of the essence of worship.

GATHERING SONGS

7
JESUS BE AMONG US

Jesus be among us in your risen power;
may we who are fearful, know your presence here;
fire imagination, kindle faithful prayer,
rouse our sluggish senses to discern you here.

Ever present Spirit, move among us now,
raise our expectations by your gentle power;
lift our timid voices, tune discordant hearts,
that our time of worship may your life impart.

Tune: Houghton TiS 190

To an older generation, the first line of this hymn may have echoes of 'an old favourite' from the *Methodist Hymn Book*. But the value of new words to familiar tunes is that more modern words and phrases, together with a different tune, can change the tone, and even the meaning, of a hymn. The words reflect everyday language expressing divine aspirations. These new words are set to music that was originally a French country dance melody.

8
WE GATHER TOGETHER

We gather together to ask for God's blessing
to worship and praise him in word and with song;
for God's our creator and we are his creatures,

> *O praise to the Almighty*
> *Sing praise to our God!*

We gather together to listen for God's Word,
be open to listen to what God would say;
in Jesus the Saviour, that Word has been spoken,

> *O praise to the Almighty*
> *Sing praise to our God!*

We gather together so we may be nourished,
be served by God's Spirit, in bread and with wine;
that God should so bless us, to share in his own life,

> *O praise to the Almighty*
> *Sing praise to our God!*

We gather together and then we are sent out
empowered by the Spirit to serve humankind;
in our daily living we share in God's mission,

> *O praise to the Almighty*
> *Sing praise to our God!*

Tune: 'Kremser' (TiS 107)

The first line of this hymn is taken from a Christian hymn of Dutch origin written in 1597 by Adrianus Valerius. The chorus is borrowed from Paulus Gerhardt's hymn ('Sing praise and thanksgiving...' TiS 107). It is suitable as a gathering hymn for the beginning of worship, reminding the congregation that we come to worship not as individuals, seeking private blessings, but to be served as a community by God through Word and Sacraments.

HYMNS OF PRAISE

Magpies

Magpies carolling
the dawning of a new day
sing praise

HYMNS OF PRAISE

Magpies caroling,
the dawning of a new day
sing praise

9
A HYMN OF PRAISE

Glory be to God Creator
and to the incarnate Son,
and to the eternal Spirit
blessed three and holy One.

God who fully condescended
to our frail humanity,
born of Mary, living simply,
glory for your poverty.

Jesus Christ who through his dying
unmasked evil's artifice,
yielding to our base conniving,
glory for your sacrifice.

Holy Spirit from the Father
guiding us through history,
through all trials and tribulations
bring us to your promised end.

> Tune 'Marching' TiS 165

The beginning of a community's worship is usually a call to acknowledge the presence of God with a song of praise. This turns our focus towards the God who has promised to meet us here. Praise directed to God is not done for its effect on ourselves as seems the case in some churches where 'praise' is emphasised. Neither is praise an activity that 'warms up' the congregation. Something vital is missing if our worship is focused only on ourselves. We might describe it as 'awe' in God's presence. This hymn directs us to who God is and what God has done for us in Christ.

10
GLORY BE TO GOD

Glory be to God Creator
and to the incarnate Son,
and to the eternal Spirit
blessed three and holy one.
Glory, glory, glory, glory
praise the holy trinity.

God who fully condescended
to our frail humanity,
born of Mary, living simply,
glory for your poverty.
Glory, glory, glory, glory
God made flesh with us to dwell.

Jesus Christ who through his dying
unmasked evil's artifice,
conquering our base conniving,
glory for your sacrifice.
Glory, glory, glory, glory
for your victory on the cross.

Holy Spirit from the Father
brooding o'er Creation's night,
joining us to Jesus' victory
raising us to heaven's height.
Glory, glory, glory, glory
for your resurrection light.

Tune: 'Regent Square' TiS 142

This hymn celebrates the foundational Christian doctrines of who God is, what God has done through Jesus Christ and the ongoing work of the Holy Spirit in bringing us, and the Creation, to God's chosen end. My hope is to offer a nourishing and joyful trinitarian song of praise with a singable theology.

11
THE GOD OF HISTORY

The Banyule Network Hymn

Gracious God, whose faithful presence
led your people on their way
out of slavery into freedom
and the hope of a new day,
be with us who tread uncertain
from the safety of the past,
grant us faith and hope to trust in
your sure love until the last.

Brother Jesus, who has called us
to be followers of your way,
fashioned us to be a people,
your own body here today.

As we move beyond our comfort
keep us focused on your call;
boldly living out our witness
daring though we fail and fall.

Holy Spirit, God here with us,
gentle agent of the Son:
may we know your powerful presence
working so God's will is done.
Lead us to your promised future,
strengthen us for ministry,
confident that you are with us,
trusting where we cannot see.

Tunes: Gaelic Air TiS 477 or Ode to Joy TiS 152

> This hymn was written for the Banyule Network of Uniting Churches Covenanting Service on 23 November 2008. Six congregations covenanted together to share their resources to be more effective in the Church's mission and service within the Banyule Municipality. The Network continues to grow and change in the spirit of this hymn.

12
WE PRAISE YOU, GOD

Dedicated to the Ormond Uniting Church congregation: 21 August 1990

We praise you, God Creator,
by whose almighty Word
the world and all things living
out of your love were formed;
with mother love your nurture
gathers within your grace
the fragile, wild creation
and all the human race.

We praise you, God of Sarah,
who bore the promised son,
the mother of a nation,
Israel, elected one.
Out of that pilgrim people,
the Servant of the Lord,
was born the promised Saviour
Jesus, incarnate Word.

We praise you, God the Father,
through Jesus Christ your Son,
that by the Holy Spirit,
we are with him made one;
humanity made perfect for woman
as for man,
not counting on our merits but
what for us he's won.

We praise you, God the Spirit,
our Comforter and friend,
God present in our living
God waiting at our end.
Yours is the truth and mission
we serve and celebrate,
in joy and hope and freedom
your Kingdom we await.

We praise you, God all faithful,
love source of all the saints,
the Church's guide through history,
her strength before Hell's gates;
'tis you alone will bring us
into your promised land,
where your renewed creation
will praise you without end.

Tune: 'Cruger' TiS 202

> When I was a Minister of the Word in the Ormond U.C. congregation, I was often inspired by the people's singing, especially during the first hymn of praise that began the worship. One week, I was looking for a 'big' hymn that celebrated God's dealings with God's people through history but could find nothing in *The Australian Hymn Book* that seemed suitable to me. I worked on this hymn during the week and we sang it that Sunday morning. A hymn born of their devotion and so dedicated to that congregation.

CONFESSION and FORGIVENESS

Black Swan

Gliding blackly,
at peace
in her forgiveness

CONFESSION and FORGIVENESS

13
NO CONDEMNATION NOW
Romans 8:1-17

No condemnation now
for those who dare believe
what God has done in Jesus Christ,
sin's captives are set free.

The law of sin and death
is overcome by One
who came to us in our own flesh
the Father's only Son.

He only could fulfil
what was required by law,
condemning sin in his own flesh,
he gifted life to all.

The Spirit makes it so,
the One who dwells within,
who raises us to life with Christ
and breaks the power of sin.

So let us set our minds
on what the Spirit gives
and be content to live in Christ
whose gifts are life and peace.

In praise we cry 'Abba'
and claim our destiny,
as heirs with the Lord Jesus Christ,
we share his life in heaven.

Tune: St Michael, TiS 483

This hymn celebrates the great gospel affirmation in Romans 8 that in Jesus Christ, God has set humanity free from the power of sin and death. It is a respectful echo of verses in Charles Wesley's great hymn *'And can it be that I should gain an interest in the Saviour's blood.'* TiS 209

14
WE ARE FORGIVEN

To be sung after the Declaration of Forgiveness

Did you hear the proclamation?
Has the word lodged in your heart?
God declares you are forgiven
all your sins are cleared away.
Every wrong you have committed,
unforgettable regret;
sins and torments, pain and failure
which deny, malign your worth.

These are taken from your shoulders
Jesus bore them on the tree;
in this wonderful transaction
God, by grace, has set us free.
When we stand to hear the verdict
on that final Judgment Day,
this, the word that shall be spoken,
'Welcome, friend, you are forgiven'.

Tune: Abbot's Leigh TiS 446

For the congregation at Highfield Road Uniting Church

This hymn originated as a reflection on a Prayer of Confession offered in my home congregation. The Declaration of Forgiveness which follows the prayer in the liturgy is an early proclamation of the Gospel. After confessing to God our human brokenness and sin, the Presider makes the declaration: 'In Jesus Christ, your sins are forgiven'. The traditional response by the congregation is, 'Thanks be to God'. In my experience, few congregations give this response the joyful and liberating response the proclamation deserves. Our liberation from sin into the freedom of Christian faith deserves more conviction than what is often given by the people. The hymn seeks to clarify why it is possible and deserving of a more enthusiastic response.

PRAYER

Wedge Tail Eagle

On the wings of prayer
we rise,
soaring into the heavens

PRAYER

We are all eagle.
On the wings of prayer
we rise
soaring into the heavens.

15
A LAMENT
after Psalm 6

In loneliness my heart cries out,
my soul in sorrow faints;
anger, it fires my trembling bones
and outrage sears my soul.

Where are you God in my despair?
Can you deliver me?
My prayers to you fly out unheard
from haunts of loneliness.

I weary with my moaning cries
I flood my bed with tears;
I drown my eyes with weeping sighs
and no one hears my prayers.

O turn, O Lord, and save my life,
deliver me through grace;
for in the depths of Sheol
how shall I sing your praise?

Tune: Belmont TiS 514

Psalm 6 appears to be written as a prayer of a sick person seeking physical healing. The inference is that Yahweh is the origin of the illness. This hymn accepts the person is battling their own mortality and trusts that the grace of the God of Jesus Christ will deliver them from a final alienation.

16
AS JESUS TAUGHT US
[The Lord's Prayer versified]

Holy and eternal God,
Jesus called 'Our Father',
honour to that name we bring,
praise your wholly otherness.

Here and now your kingdom come
to renew creation;
may your holy will be done,
here on earth as 'tis in heav'n.

Grant us food we need today,
for our body's nourishment;
may we share with all in need
from earth's wealthy providence.

When your way we choose to shun
grant us your forgiveness please;
give us grace to forgive those
whom we name as enemies.

Save us when the evil powers
bring us to the brink of death;
when the time of suff'ring comes,
grant us your deliverance.

Yours the reign that stands alone,
when all time comes to an end;
Suff'ring love is shown to be,
kingdom, power and the glory.

Suggested Tune: 'Vienna' TiS 440

> The Lord's Prayer has become so familiar to people that it is often recited thoughtlessly. The meaning of what we are doing in obedience to Jesus' command is lost. My hope is that by versifying Jesus' prayer and singing rather than reciting, people may hear the words with refreshed significance.

17
JESUS, SON OF MARY

Jesus, Son of Mary, God's Word in our flesh,
fashioned in our likeness, born to take our part;
hear the words we offer, spoken from the heart,
we believe that through you, every prayer is heard.

Holy Spirit helper, listen to our plea,
hear the groans we utter, let the Father see,
not our flimsy goodness, nor our poverty,
but the grace of Jesus, crucified for me.

Gracious God mysterious, holy Trinity,
you whose love we've trusted, where we cannot see;
take the lives we offer, broken though they be,
show your glory through our mere humanity.

Tune: *Au clair de la lune* TiS 236

> In worship, we often get caught up in our own work and our needs and forget the work of the Triune God. This hymn seeks to give us words that acknowledge that our words are offered 'through Jesus Christ'. It proclaims that Jesus is our Intercessor before God [Hebrews 4:14-16]. This means that the Holy Spirit carries our prayers into the presence of God; that God receives us as we are and uses us as vehicles of God's grace.

18

WHO AM I

after Psalm 131

God, who am I that I can come to you
with heavy heart and burdens I must bear?
I have no right to raise my eyes to heaven,
nor means to know the mystery of your ways.

But I have stilled my soul in quietness,
rested my head against your breast in peace;
with mother love, you hold me tenderly,
in your embrace there's nothing I should fear.

O child of God, trust in this mother love;
flee to her arms in your most dire distress,
and there in safety find your truest hope,
freedom from fear both now and evermore.

Tune: Sursum Corda TiS 240

Psalm 131 is one of many passages in the First Testament where the relation of Yahweh and Israel is likened to parent and child. This psalm appealed to me because of the simile of a child and its mother coming before God in hope. The person does not come with arrogance, sure of their right to approach God, but as one who has no hope but the faithfulness and love of God. The image of being held securely in the arms of mother God seems very strong to me. The hymn has the feel of a lullaby. It could be used artfully before the prayers of confession or the prayers for others.

PROCLAMATION

Brolga

Caught up in good news
with wonder and abandon
the Brolga dances

19
GIFT OF GRACE
(Romans 3:19-31)

1. Praise be to God who proves his righteousness;
praise be to Jesus Christ, God's only Son;
and praises to the Holy Trinity,
whose gracious work has our salvation won.

2. Since all have sinned and fallen short of God
and failed to live God's vital righteousness,
what hope is there for any human soul
to be delivered from this hopelessness?

3. Thanks be to God who's given us a way,
redemption through the life of Christ the Son,
whose perfect life is offered up for all,
God's own self-giving breaks the power of sin.

4. God's justice is expressed in righteousness,
God's willingness to justify all those
who trust in Jesus as God's means of grace,
a gift to be received by faith alone.

5. There are no godly works to be achieved
no pious acts which we can proudly boast;
we dare to trust the way that God provides
and claim the gift of faith in Jesus Christ.

*6. Praise be to God who proves his righteousness;
praise be to Jesus Christ, God's only Son;
and praises to the Holy Trinity
whose gracious work has our salvation won.*

Tune: Sursum Corda TiS 240

Paul's letter to the Romans contains some of the most developed theology of the heart of the gospel in the New Testament. This hymn reflects on salvation as a gift of God, an accomplishment of the life, death and resurrection of Jesus which people receive through trust (faith) in what God has done. This hymn may come as a surprise to some churchgoers.

20

THE APOSTLES' CREED

(versified)

The Church's faith through ages
is summed up in a creed;
that all who follow Jesus
may have a guiding light.
We say that God Almighty,
the holy trinity
created earth and heaven,
and mysteries beyond.

We hold that Jesus Christ was
the Son of God made flesh,
born of a human mother
he lived as one of us;
subjected to earth's powers
of Temple, power and law,
was crucified and buried
and laid down with the dead.

By act of new creation,
God raised him up from death;
restored him to God's glory
as Lord and Judge of earth;
we trust the Holy Spirit,
the Church with all her saints,
forgiveness, resurrection
and everlasting life.

This basic affirmation,
a light and not a law,
directs our hopes to Jesus
through whom this God we know.
This faith is our salvation
not by our right belief,
but through our simple trust in
what God has done for us.

Tune 'Aurelia' TiS 457 76. 76.D

The Apostles' Creed is a succinct statement of the foundational beliefs of the ancient church that have nurtured the Church since the beginning. It can continue to enlighten God's Church and give us a place to stand as we wrestle with the pressing issues of our contemporary culture and time. My hope is that by singing this Creed we may again learn to delight in its wisdom.

SACRAMENTS

Welcome Swallow

Welcome! cried Swallow;
There is room for everyone
here, at the table

SACRAMENTS

We're mot Smellier

..... welcome cried Sw allow!
There is room for everyone
here... at the table.

SACRAMENTS

21
NEW LIFE IN CHRIST
(Romans 6:5-6)

Before you, God, we dare to sing,
    your grace gives us a voice,
when on your mercy we reflect
    we cannot but rejoice.

Our God, you call us by our name
    the cross on us is signed
and you have named us as your own,
    in Christ our self we find.

You wash us clean of all our sin,
    our old life washed away;
you raise us up, new born to live
    towards your coming day.

Christ's robe of righteousness we wear
    to clothe our nakedness,
so we can stand before your throne
    secure in your own grace.

The Spirit works the miracle,
    by word and sign it's done
and we engrafted to the church
    are family with your Son.

Before you, God, we dare to sing
    your grace gives us a voice,
when on your mercy we reflect
    we cannot but rejoice.

Suggested Tune: Lucius TiS 442ii
Alternative Tune: Jackson TiS 563

This hymn was the winner of Section 2 (original words to existing music) of the 2013 Australian Hymn Book Pty Ltd International Hymn Competition

> This hymn celebrates the gift of baptism as a sacrament that unites a person to Christ and clothes them with the faith of Jesus. Many metaphors in Scripture describe this transaction but this one uses words from Romans 6:5-6.

22
SHALL WE GATHER AT THE TABLE

Shall we gather at the table
where the Lord of life presides?
Here the blessed food of heaven
hides within the bread and wine.

Refrain: *Yes, we'll gather at the table*
come by grace with all the saints together
gather by faith around the table
to feast on the food of God.

Shall we gather at the table
though our hands are soiled by sin?
Trusting in the grace of Jesus
that washes clean our every stain.

Refrain

Shall we gather at the table
though we have no right to come?
Jesus was known as friend of sinners
he gives us his own welcome.

Refrain

Shall we gather at the table
though we have not proper dress?
He who died upon the cross though
clothes us with his righteousness.

Refrain

Tune: Shall we gather at the river
Tune available in Alexander's Hymns No 3 #86]

This well-known American gospel song ('At the River') was originally written as a hymn titled 'Beautiful River' written in 1864 by American poet and gospel music composer Robert Lowry. I have rewritten the words as a communion song and hope that congregations may sing it in 'gospel style'. I intend it as a corrective to the dearth of eucharistic hymns that express joy and thanksgiving for our being at the table of the Lord. I think we have an excessive focus on blood and sacrifice and mournful tunes in our eucharistic liturgies.

DISCIPLESHIP

Flame Robin

A red flame flickers
amidst green leaves,
small sign of Spirit and life

23
JESUS WAS A STRANGER

Jesus was a stranger and a refugee,
forced to leave his country, with his family;
sent away from home by government decree,
Jesus was a stranger and a refugee.

Jesus sought asylum in a far country;
from a murd'rous tyrant he was forced to flee;
wandering down to Egypt, holy family,
looking for a place of hospitality.

I see you, Lord Jesus, in this homeless band;
yours the eyes of migrants forced to flee their land;
you're the mother grieving in the desert sand;
yours the supplication in her outstretched hand.

Give to me the grace, God, not to turn away,
nor to turn a blind eye, when I bow to pray;
open up our hearts, Lord, free your church to say,
you are welcome, stranger, join us in God's name.

Tune: *Au clair de la lune* (TiS 236)

This hymn was originally published in *Something to Sing About: 11 Songs that celebrate being a multicultural Church*; Published by National Assembly Multicultural and Cross-cultural Ministry 2005

> This hymn is based on the story of Jesus' birth and early life from chapter 2 of the Gospel of Matthew. It has many of the features of the experience of refugees and asylum seekers in our own time and another example of ways in which God in Christ identifies with the poor, the outcast and those on the margins of their societies. It is entirely consistent with the life, teaching and experience of Jesus of Nazareth.

24
LOVE IS SERVICE

O Father, Son and Spirit one
in common love, a mystery,
you draw us to your life divine
and feed us with Christ's bread and wine.

O give us, Lord, a generous heart,
a graciousness shaped by your own,
a lavish generosity
that shares your love for land and town.

O grant us, Saviour of the world,
a passion for your mission here,
a knowledge of your truthful word
and courage to confront our fear.

Go with us Spirit, to the world,
empower us by your presence there,
to serve all people with your Word
and willing, too, his cross to bear.

So may our work in ministry
be shaped like Christ's in deed and word,
that all the world may learn your truth,
your name alone be glorified.

Tune: Melcombe TiS 213 (ii)

The early Methodists learned their faith through the singing of the Wesleys' (and others') hymns. It was a truism that 'Methodism was born in song'. One of the aims of my hymn writing is to try and put the doctrine of the Christian Faith into singable, teachable language. In this hymn, the simple conviction that all Christian service finds its roots in the God who serves the world by entering into its life and sharing it wholly and redemptively.

25
O GOD, FORGIVE

O God, forgive our thankless ways,
our lack of grace towards all life,
the secret sin, the pride of heart,
the source of human sin and strife.

O give us, Lord, a generous heart,
a graciousness to match your own,
an open-hearted selflessness
to share your love for humankind.

O grant us, Saviour of the world,
a passion for your mission here,
a knowledge of your truthful word
and courage to confront our fear.

O Father, Son and Spirit, one
in common love, a mystery,
you draw us to your life divine
and feed us with Christ's bread and wine.

Go with us, Lord, into the world
that we may be your presence there,
to serve all people with your Word
and willingness your cross to bear.

Tune: Gonfalon Royal TiS 332

This hymn sings the truth that 'we love God because God first loved us' [1 John 4:19]. It sings the desire that we may be faithful disciples who know the gospel truth that we are forgiven sinners. We ask God to equip us so we may be those through whom the light of Christ shines in our everyday living.

26
O GOD OF LOVE AND JUSTICE

O God of love and justice,
you hold in your embrace
the marvellous diversity
of all the human race;
wherever love for others
is motive for the deed
your love, O God, is present,
love is your only creed.

O God of love and justice,
whose judgment is your love,
'tis not your wrath and anger
from which our hearts would move,
but that your love would welcome
poor sinners such as we.
is way beyond our usual
be-live-a-bil-ity.

O God of love and justice,
your heart goes out to all;
the sinner and the sinned against
how easily we judge;
the worthy and the worthless,
oppressor and oppressed,
are loved by you all equally;
so scandalous your love.

O God of love and justice,
save us from human pride
that judges others' efforts
and their mistakes deride,
or covers gross injustice
with apathetic love,
expecting all that's needed
will fall down from above.

O God of love and justice,
may we all faithfully
bear witness to your love and
your justice equally,
that in our life together,
the people of your way
may live the coming Kingdom,
signs of your glorious day.

Tune: Ellacombe TiS 361

> This hymn is an affirmation that the mission of God in the world requires the Church's commitment to both love **and** justice. It is found in the message of the prophets and in the ministry of Jesus' life and teaching. Too often, though, the Church has failed to keep together these twin responsibilities of the mission of the people of God.

27
THE CALL TO DISCIPLESHIP
(after Mark 1:16-20)

1. The Lord of life goes walking by
the salty sea shore of our lives;
he watches us at daily work,
we're unprepared for his surprise.

2. He speaks to us in gentle tones
and offers no false promises;
he simply says, 'come, follow me',
to learn to live the way he says.

3. But every time I've had to choose,
it seemed his way was not for me;
I'd planned my path, set my own goals
to build a dream that I could see.

4. But then he sought me out again,
so gracious is his patient love;
he called me to discipleship
to learn to shape my life to his.

5. I follow now this Lord of life,
my heart attuned to human pain;
serving the last, the least, the lost,
off-er-ing hope in Jesus' name.

6. So every day I make the choice
to live his way of grace and peace,
showing in deed through daily life
the truth of what God promises.

Tune: O Waly, Waly TiS 654

Being Christian involves responding to the call of Jesus to be his disciple, learning to live his way in everyday life. It is not membership of an organisation but a daily commitment to live a human life shaped by his teachings and presence.

In Memoriam: Bruce Alcorn (1942-2020): A friend from youth group days; passionate Double Bass player; active indigenous advocate; Cystic Fibrosis administrator, who sent me the music of popular songs to make words for hymns.

BLESSING and DISMISSAL

Sulphur Crested Cockatoo

Flying unconstrained,
its raucous song of freedom calls us
to embrace our own

28
A LIFE THAT SINGS

God, be our companion
in the days ahead;
help our lives be worthy
and by Jesus led.

May your Holy Spirit
guide us in all things,
so our daily living
shows a life that sings.

Tune: North Coates TiS 600 (ii)

In sociology, 'embodiment' is defined as the giving of human form to a spirit. In a Christian sense, it is the belief that each Christian is a part of the Body of Christ through their baptism. Who we are and what we do in our daily lives is giving human form to the Spirit of Jesus in our world. Worship forms us to know how to be the Body of Christ through the actions of our human bodies. The metaphor of 'a life that sings' is a multi-faceted metaphor for those things that reveal Jesus to others and affirms their humanness as beloved of God.

29
GO WITH US, LORD

Go with us, Lord, to tread our road ahead,
be our companion in our times of dread;
and if we stumble your Word to believe
give strength and courage that we persevere.

For your strong Spirit constantly is near
and gives us heart to overcome our fear;
thus, may our lives bear witness to your grace
and people see in ours, your loving face.

Tune: Chilton Foliat TiS 487

This hymn reminds the members of a congregation of the resources gifted to them by the Holy Spirit as they go from the gathering for worship to their individual lives of discipleship. They go as living embodiments of the gospel in the variety of their vocations and Christian service. That is often tough work in these times, but we are assured we are not alone in doing it.

ADVENT and CHRISTMAS

Superb Fairy Wren

A tiny presence
in blue and fawn
proclaiming their resilience

30
ADVENT/CHRISTMAS DOXOLOGY

Praise God who honoured human worth
submitting to an earthly birth.
Praise God who came to share our life,
embracing human care and strife.

Praise God whose coming in the Son
brings gifts of *hope/love/joy/peace/life to everyone.
Praise God one holy Trinity
with whom we share community.

Tune: Fairhill TiS 768 (i) or Old Hundredth TiS 768 (ii)

Appropriate word to be sung during the lighting of Advent candles and in the Christmas season.

> The unrelenting jollity of our cultural Christmas finds a welcome respite when the Church sings and celebrates the incomprehensible truth of the Christ-mass message—'The Word became flesh and dwelt among us full of grace and truth' (John 1:14). When all is said and done, Christmas joy is based on the fact that God has come among us as a human being so that we may know God's nature and purpose in a way that we can comprehend, through space, time and matter.

31
JOSEPH'S CAROL
Matthew 1:18-25

We sing the praise of Mary
in carol, song and hymn,
but what of humble Joseph
is there no song for him?

In Matthew's Gospel we hear told
of this just, righteous man
when faced with scandal fear and shame
protected Mary's name.

He hears the angel's quiet call
and bravely trusts that word
to marry Mary, and become
a father to her child.

Now Mary had a family home
through what Joseph had done,
and Jesus had a step-father
and David's line, a son.

In this forgotten figure stands
a strong and silent man,
who though he had no words to say
was faithful to obey.

So sing the praise of Joseph,
the man often ignored,
whose masculine obedience
was model for our Lord.

Tune: Kilmarnock TiS 247

> Joseph's importance to Mary's vocation is largely ignored in the Scriptures, but is humanly critical for Mary and her child in a patriarchal society. I wanted a hymn that recognised Joseph's faithful love of Mary and their strange son that enabled both Mary and Jesus to fulfil their destiny. It is interesting to reflect on how their humanity might have formed that of the man Jesus.

32
THE CHILD JESUS
(Luke 2:41-51)

Infant Jesus as a child
cradled by his mother,
grew in wisdom, stature, strength,
just like any other.
As he grew into a youth
Jesus was rebellious,
foll'wing his own inner light,
disobeyed his parents.

Once, while in Jerusalem,
Jesus' parents lost him;
then had to retrace their steps,
anxious for his safety.
Then, to their astonishment,
found him in the Temple
with the scholars of the Law
seeking understanding.

To their loving chastisement
Jesus told them boldly,
'Why did you all look for me
in your anxious searching?
Did you not expect I'd be
in my Father's Temple?'
But his parents failed to see
what the boy was meaning.

Luke alone records this scene
of the Saviour's childhood;
in this homely episode
truth is clearly spoken;
Jesus shows that God with us
shares our human journey,
as a baby, child and man
he redeems us wholly.

Tune: Good King Wenceslas [*public domain*]
[*or in* Hymns for Today's Church #145]

It was common practice in the 18th and 19th centuries for hymn writers and musicians to 'borrow' tunes from secular sources to do service as tunes for hymns.

Good King Wenceslas celebrates a Duke of Bohemia (907–935 CE) who gave alms to the poor. The carol was written in 1853 by John Mason Neale and the melody is an 13th century tune called 'Tempus adest floridum' in praise of the Spring. Here I have turned it into a hymn that celebrates an incident in the childhood of Jesus only recorded in Luke's gospel. The hymn shows a side of his divine/human nature that we rarely contemplate.

33
WHAT CHILD IS THIS

What child is this whose life began
so wondrously, so mysteriously
whose birth would threaten kings and thrones
and draw the wonder of wise ones?

> *This, this is God made flesh*
> *our God among us dwelling;*
> *God, a child in human form*
> *Jesus the son of Mary*

What child is this who draws the wrath
of a tyrant bent on genocide?
In face of evil forced to flee
as refugees compelled to hide.

> *This, this is Christ the strange,*
> *friend of outcasts and refugees,*
> *God no stranger to our ways,*
> *Christ the Son of Mary.*

What child is this grown to a man
whose teaching is unsettling;
who riles the leaders of the law
provoking those in power?

> *This, this is Christ the seer*
> *prophet, preacher of God's news;*
> *a message for all who turn to hear*
> *the news of grace in his gospel.*

What man is this who meets his end
in public execution,
brought low by evil powers intent
on causing love's destruction?

> *This, this is Christ the king*
> *embracing all that death could bring*
> *choosing the way of suffering*
> *the crucified Son of Mary.*

Tune: Greensleeves [see *Hymns for Todays Church* #145 or public domain]

My hymn is a rewriting of 'What child is this' by William Chatterton Dix, a hymn first published in 1871. It appeared in *The Australian Hymn Book* (1977) but is not in *Together in Song* (1999). My rewriting makes use of Chatterton Dix's literary structure but uses different language, metaphors and images to tell the story of the incarnation of God into human life and history. Based firmly on the biblical texts, it seeks to draw the meaning of Jesus birth into the world and issues of the 21st century.

The hymn may be sung with half the congregation singing the question, the other half the response, or by using a cantor or choir in the same way.

LECTIONARY SONGS

Ravens

Unappreciated
but resolute;
they keep turning up

34
TRANSFIGURATION SONG
(for children)

Jesus shone in glorious light
giving followers a fright.
When they saw him shining so
they did not know what to do.

From the light they heard a voice
telling them who Jesus was;
'This is my beloved Son,
listen what he says to you'.

Peter said, 'Lord, let us stay
on this mountain top all day.
I will build three booths for you
Moses and Elijah too'.

'No', said Jesus, 'Let us go
to the people down below;
with the lost and suffering ones
is the place for God's own Son'.

Tune: Vienna: TiS 440

> This story of the strange experience of Jesus and three of his disciples on the mountain can have a particular appeal to children who usually enjoy mysteries. The hymn declares Jesus to be a special person who reveals God to be one who comes among human beings in order to serve them with God's grace.

35
EVENING PRAYER

Watch with us waking, dear Saviour, we pray,
you have walked with us throughout the long day;
guide us while waking and guard us asleep
bring us in safety through night's unknown deep.

Tune: Slane TiS 547

Fear of the night time is a common anxiety of children and those who are sick or troubled. It is a helpful discipline to offer prayer to God before going to sleep. The words of this hymn use an image from the Service for Compline in the Anglican *Book of Common Prayer*. It may be recited individually or sung communally and become one of those prayers we could helpfully know by heart.

36
ASCENSION INTROIT

As the church together
gathered round the Word,
seeing in each other
Christ the human Lord:
free our earth-bound reason,
lift our stone-cold hearts
so we may give glory
to the risen One.

Tune: *Camberwell* 65.65 D TiS 231

The Feast of the Ascension is celebrated on one day in the Christian calendar, on a Thursday. That means it is often overlooked in the Sunday worship of congregations. However, in our times when power and dominion feature so largely in the political and social affairs of our world, it is a useful way for teaching and honouring what power and dominion means in the Christian faith. To feature the theological meaning of the Ascension in the Church's worship on the Sunday after Ascension is an opportunity to relate faith and culture. This little Introit could well introduce the worship for that day.

37
HOLY SPIRIT FIRE #1

1. Before the ancient dreaming time,
God's Spirit brought to birth
and gifted our first peoples
the fire that nurtures earth.
In time of Exodus, God gave
a sign of cloud by day;
and then a sign of fire by night
to guide them in God's way.

2. At Pentecost, the Spirit's fire
alighted on each head
and kindled in uncertain hearts
a gospel fire instead.
Good news of Jesus died and risen
like swift wildfire was spread
by witnesses in every age
igniting heart and head.

3. And so today, warm-hearted God,
set lives and hearts on fire
as witnesses before the world
your truth fuels our desire.
The truth to challenge cruel power
yet whisper 'you are mine'
to all among the lost and least
a blazing Kingdom sign.

4. Bright Spirit, may your life bring forth
the hope no power can end
and bring the whole creation home
to light and joy in heaven.
All praise to our Creator God
and our Redeemer Friend,
all praises to the Spirit now
and evermore. Amen.

Tune: Tyrolese TiS 235

Written for and sung at the 14th Assembly of the UCA, Perth 2016

> A hymn that uses the ancient symbol of fire for the activity of the Triune God in human history.

> This song is also offered in a different metre with an extra half verse and a different effect at #38 in Songs in Season..

38
HOLY SPIRIT FIRE #2

1. Before the ancient dreaming time
God's Spirit brought to birth
a land for our first peoples and
the fire to nurture earth.

2. In time of Exodus, God gave
a sign of cloud by day
and then a sign of fire by night
to guide them in God's way.

3. At Pentecost, the Spirit's fire
alighted on each head
and kindled in uncertain hearts
a gospel fire instead.

4. Good news of Jesus died and risen
like swift wildfire was spread
by witnesses in every age
igniting heart and head.

5. And so today, warm-hearted God,
set lives and hearts on fire
as witnesses before the world
your truth fuels our desire.

6. The truth to challenge cruel power
and whisper 'you are mine'
to all among the lost and least
a blazing Kingdom sign.

7. Bright Spirit may your life bring forth
the hope no power can end
and bring the whole creation home
to light and joy in heav'n.

Tune: St Peter TiS 485

SONGS IN SEASON

Written for and sung at the 14th Assembly of the UCA, Perth 2016

> A hymn that uses the ancient symbol of fire for the activity of the Triune God in human history. It could be used especially during the season of Pentecost.

39
PENTECOST INVOCATION

As we gather here together
wondering what next will be,
let us listen to the wind's song
breath of Pentecost in me.

Holy Spirit, gift of Jesus,
come upon us with your power,
reassure us of Christ's presence,
drawing in your gentle breath.

If our fear and apprehension
causes us to doubt God's truth;
stimulate imagination,
bring our dormant hearts to life.

Tune: Omni Die TiS 101

After the news of Jesus' resurrection, the uncertain disciples gathered in an upper room waiting to see what would happen next. Centuries later, Jesus' disciples do the same. Uncertain and afraid, we too often fail to recognise the presence of the Holy Spirit who enlivens as the Spirit of the risen One. The hymn is a prayer for that gift that still enlivens the heart, mind and soul of assembled disciples.

40
THROUGH THE ARTISTRY OF CHILDREN

Through the artistry of children
and their wonder, fresh and free,
may we see with clearer vision,
Jesus, your nativity.

Mindful of the awesome wonder
of the God who's born a child,
we delight to see in person
God among us in disguise.

May their songs our joy awaken,
shake us from propriety,
help us see God's holy presence
in a child's simplicity.

In their plain participation,
we perceive them off'ring praise,
so they join our joyful voices
and the Church's song is raised.

Tune: 'Sharon' TiS # 140 or 'Omni Die' TiS # 101

In Jesus' teaching in the Gospels, he holds up a child as a model of the disciple [e.g. Matthew 18:3]. In the children present in the Christian community there is a living reminder of how God has chosen to be among us. In their total dependence on being accepted by grace and not achievement, they are models for all disciples. The scarcity of children in many modern congregations is a loss for the whole community of this reminder of the basis of our acceptance by God.

INDEX OF HYMN TUNES
from TOGETHER IN SONG and SEASONS IN SONG

Tune	TiS	SiS
Abbot's Leigh	446	14
Au Claire de La Lune	236	7, 17, 23
Aurelia	457	20
Belmont	514	15
Camberwell	231	23
Chilton Foliat	487	28
Cruger	202	12
Ellacombe	361	26
Fairhill	768 (i)	31
Franconia	490	1
Fulda	608	34
Gaelic Air	477	12
Glenfinlas	600 (i)	6
Gonfalon Royal	332	35
Houghton	190	7
Jackson	563	21
Kilmarnock	247	37
Kremser	107	8
Lucius	442 (ii)	21
Marching	165	9
Melcome	213 (ii)	24
North Coates	600 (ii)	5
Ode to Joy	152	12
Old Hundredth	769 (ii)	31
Omni Die	101	7, 17, 23
O Waly, Waly	654	27
Regent Square	142	10

81

SONGS IN SEASON

Sharon	140	39
Slane	547	32
St Denio	143	4
St Michael	483	13
St Peter	485	36
Sursum Corda	240	18, 19
Tyrolese	235	36
Vienna	440	16

SOURCES FOR OTHER TUNES

At the River [Tune available in 'Alexander Hymns No 3 #86]

Good King Wenceslas [Hymns for Today's Church #145: Published by Hodder & Stoughton; 1982]

Greensleeves: [available in the public domain]

www.ingramcontent.com/pod-product-compliance
Lightning Source LLC
Chambersburg PA
CBHW012007090526
44590CB00026B/3911